Dedicated to my son Nick.

Who explores the rivers and streams watching and learning in the presences of fish, tree's and all of God's creatures.

Summary
Photographs of animals that use camouflage to help them hide from predation. Samantha Rhymes uses lyrical rhymes to help show young naturalist where and how to discover new animals. Each page holds facts about the animal or their environment.

Rhymedog LLC   2015

For information regarding permission to reproduce any part of this book,email S.Rhymes and associated logos and trademark.
Printed in U.S.A Createspace
First edition September 2016
Library of Congress Cataloging-in-Publication Data
Rhymes,S 2015
Rhymedog/S. Rhymes

Animal fact, Salmon fry and alevin. The salmon spawning grounds are backwater streams and rivers. After 2 to 6 months the eggs hatch into tiny larvae called sac fry or alevin. The alevin has a sac containing the remainder of the yolk.

Rhymedogg LLC 2015
srhymesdogg@gmail.com

<u>Look, Look</u>
<u>Can You See Me!</u>

I am clear and bright
Hiding when its night.

My body keeps me
safe and sound.
Blending into the
forest ground.

On this tiny green
leaf face.
I eat bugs at my
own pace.

Animal Fact: Tree frogs breath through their skin
and their lungs, they can become sick if exposed to
pollutants in the air.

Can you see me on the tray?
I get scared and fly away.

Into the forest lush and green.
How I love my tropical scene.

Flying high into the sky.
Catching bugs as they go by.

Environmental Facts: Tropical rainforest is an area on earth where living creatures experience higher average rain fall and warmer temperatures.

Look Look in the forest scene
Orange wings sit in the green.

Gently flapping in the light
Flowers fills my appetite.

My proboscis gets it done
In the tropical warm sun.

Sipping nectar is my treat
Poison skin my foe's defeat.

I am hiding in plain sight
From predation day or night.

Animal Facts: Proboscis is a tubular nose appendage that acts like a straw. Allowing butterflies to get sips of nectar from flowers.

Look Look
Can You Find Me?

Under water I hold my breath.

Traveling down to great depths.

In brackish water in disguise.

Right before your very eyes.

Environment Facts: Brackish water is salt water and fresh water mixed together.
Animal Fact: Turtle

Look ! Look !

Can you find an ocean horse.
Riding gentle on its course.

Using sea weed like a wrap.
Blending in to take a nap.

Sipping plankton by the ton.
Belly's full now were done.

Animal Facts: Weedy Sea Dragon's are fish that live off south and east Australia. Leafy and weedy sea dragons are closely related to seahorses and pipefish.

Animal Facts: Speckled Sanddabs are flatfish in the flounder family. They have both eyes on the left side of their heads.

Look Look
Can You Find Me?

Something's fishy in the sand.

Amongst the tiny grains of land.

Four eyes watch for a quick bite.

We eat crustaceans late at night.

Look Look
Can You Spy?
Floating right on bye.

**Angels drifting in the sticks.
Doing their discussing tricks.**

**Looking like their standing still.
Breathing water through their
gills.**

Animal Facts: Orinoco Angelfish, can be found in shallow lakes and slow flowing rivers in South America.

It's a thrill to see an eel.
Waiting for a fishy meal.

Spotted head and sharpen teeth.
Above the jaw and underneath.

Sleek and smooth from head to tail.
Blend right into the rocky shale.

Animal Facts: Leopard Moray eel live on tropical coral reefs. Shale is a fine-grained sedimentary rock that forms from the compaction of silt and clay-size mineral particles that we commonly call "mud."

Look look
spaceships
floating by.
Is this the ocean
or the sky.

Delicate
transparent
forms.
Surviving open
oceans storms.

Drifters collecting
a plankton treat.
Hoping for
something good
to eat.

Animal Facts:
Umbrella jelly, have short clear tentacles that
catch plankton. Jelly's can not swim and must drift
along with ocean currents and storms.

Look Look in the sea.

Changing colors it's little me.

Without bones only a single shell.

So thin and clear you can't tell.

Tentacles and special arms.

Give me all my squidy charms.

Animal Facts:
Squids have a small clear shell called a
pen. The pen is inside the body of the squid
giving it the pointed oval shape body.

Look look
Can You Find Me?

I'm in plain sight
When it is night

Blend right in
With camo skin.

Teeth they shine
Beneath the brine.

Stealth is key
Food swims to me.

Animal Facts:
Octopuses are Cephalopod's which include squid,
cuttlefish and nautilus. They are marine mollusks related
to snails and slugs. Their skin can change colors so they
blend into the environment where they live, (camouflage).

Look Look

What do you see?
In the water clear and green.
Four eyes watch this
tranquil scene.
Buoyant on the waters top
Waiting for a bug to pop.

Can you see me hanging on?
My prehensile tail is strong.

Helping when waves are rough.
When tides make swimming tough.

Animal Facts:
Sea Horses, eat small Crustacea such as Mysis shrimp.
Male sea horses are the only known animal to have true
reverse pregnancy. They carry the young in there belly
pouch.

Animal Facts: Western pond turtles, occur in marshes, streams, rivers, pond and lakes.

On a log in the sun
Catching bugs, just for fun.

In a pond with water fresh
Sitting on green algae mesh.

Carrying a shell on our back
Hide inside when predators attack.

Look, Look
Can You Spy ?

A fish thats very shy.
Dark colors on the dorsal side
Predators go by, it can hide.
Being anadromous makes me cool.
Swimming in a fishy school.

Animal Facts: Steelhead trout are anadromous. Which means these fish migrate from salt water into fresh water to spawn.

During the day we like to snooze.

Out of the sun with nothing to loose.

We wait for night when the air is cool.

Like most lizards we are no fool.

Animal Facts: Mexican beaded lizard, are venous lizards who eat birds and recital eggs. They are active at dusk till dawn.

S. Rhymes started writing lyrical rhyming stories and illustrations when she was ten. Her mom would save them in a file cabinet and bring them out to show friends and family. After retiring from teaching S. Rhymes mom told her to publish the lyrical rhyming stories. Being a good daughter Rhymes started publishing her stories under the pen name Samantha Rhymes.

www.ingramcontent.com/pod-product-compliance
Lightning Source LLC
Chambersburg PA
CBHW050759290526
45792CB00008B/2254